MAY 10, 2007

Dear Joel,

M...   ...e

of...   5

...you all your days!

Love You,
Mom
-N-
Dad

A Devoted Christian's
Prayer Book

A DEVOTED CHRISTIAN'S PRAYER BOOK

The prayers in this book have been largely selected and translated from **Die Ernsthafte Christenpflicht**, an Amish and Mennonite prayer book which dates back to 1708 or earlier. It is a collection of prayers used in daily devotions and on special occasions. Also included in this volume are the **Dortrecht Confession of Faith** of 1632 and "Rules of a Godly Life."

Pathway Publishers
Aylmer, Ontario — LaGrange, Indiana

Seventh Pathway Printing, 2003

Printed in U.S.A.

"O come, let us worship and bow down: let us kneel before the Lord our maker." Psalms 95:6.

"But the hour cometh, and now is, when the true worshipers shall worship the Father in spirit and in truth: for the Father seeketh such to worship him." John 4:23.

"Praying always with all prayer and supplication in the Spirit, and watching thereunto with all perseverance and supplication for all saints." Eph. 6:18.

"I will pray with the spirit, and I will pray with the understanding also." 1 Cor. 14:15.

THE LORD'S PRAYER

"Our Father which art in heaven, Hallowed be thy Name.

"Thy kingdom come. Thy will be done on earth, as it is in heaven.

"Give us this day our daily bread.

"And forgive us our debts, as we forgive our debtors.

"And lead us not into temptation, but deliver us from evil: for thine is the kingdom, and the power, and the glory, for ever.

Amen."

— Matthew 6:9-13

A MORNING PRAYER

O Lord, Almighty God and heavenly Father, even as Thou hast created us and given us life and placed us upon this earth to labor in trouble and sorrow until we return again to the dust from which we are taken, so hast Thou set the measure of our days that we may fear Thee and love Thee and serve Thee with our whole hearts. In Thy Fatherly goodness, Thou hast ordained the day for labor and the night for rest. So have we been refreshed by this night's repose which Thou hast so graciously bestowed upon us, and we praise Thee from the depths of our hearts for Thy watchfulness and care.

Heavenly Father, we confess that we have not always heeded Thy loving kindness, but have misused Thy gifts, disobeyed Thy commandments, and neglected our duties. With words, deeds, and thoughts we have sinned against Thee. For this, O Lord, we humbly pray Thy forgiveness, through the shed blood of Jesus Christ, Thy dear Son.

O Heavenly Father, Thou hast granted us a new day. Help us to receive it as a gift of Thy grace. Teach us the reason why Thou maketh Thy sun to shine upon us, that we may live each day according to Thy will, prepared for that approaching eternal Day.

We pray, O Holy Father, that we might leave behind the night of sin and guilt and ever walk in the shining light of Thy wondrous grace, and cast off the works of darkness, put on the armor of light, and walk honestly as in the day.

Thou God of mercy, surround us with the light of Thy love. Direct all our undertakings to Thy honor and glory. Thine eyes are flames of fire and every thought is known to Thee. We know that Thou rewardest good and punisheth evil, and therefore pray for grace to live each day in praise of Thee.

O Holy Father, even as Thou hast loved us, we pray that in love we might obey Thee. And being conscious of Thy great love toward us, we ask Thee to help us love our neighbor as ourselves. Keep us from anything that would mar this love, yea, that we might always deal honestly with our fellowmen.

Enable us to use Thy manifold blessings with moderation. Grant our hearts wisdom to avoid excess in eating and drinking and in the cares of this life. Teach us to put our trust in Thee, and to await Thy helping hand.

Give us a meek and contrite spirit, a penitent heart and true humility, yea, a hunger and thirst for Thy righteousness.

Grant us this day a pure heart, O God, to come before Thee. O Thou God and Father of love and peace, give us Thy everlasting peace and favor that we may always prove ourselves a peace-loving people, shunning all anger and malice. And give us patience to cheerfully endure any misfortune or sorrow which Thou permittest, whether a cross or tribulation, shame or suffering. O Lord, our God and Creator, direct our lives according to Thy holy will. Into Thy hands, O God, we commit ourselves, body and soul, and all our loved ones; keep us always in Thy will. We ask Thy blessings for all mankind, and especially upon those of the household of faith, wherever they may be scattered. We pray for the sick and the lonely, for those who are in sorrow, for the discouraged and the widows and the orphans. We also pray for those who would persecute and use us wrongfully. Forgive them, Lord, for they know not what they do.

We pray for the ministers of Thy church, for kings and for all that are in authority, and for all others for whom we ought to pray. O Lord, may they all receive and become partakers of Thy comfort and grace.

For this we pray, O holy Father, in the name of Thy beloved Son Jesus Christ, who has promised that Thou wilt hear us if we pray to Thee in His holy name, with devout and believing hearts. Our Father which art in heaven . . .

Thy loving countenance, O Lord, be over us by day and by night. Keep us beneath the shadow of Thy wings. Inspire, direct and bless us in all things, to Thy honor and glory. Amen.

A MORNING PRAYER

Dear God, loving heavenly Father, Thou art our Creator and Provider, under whose loving care we have enjoyed another night of rest. We praise and thank Thee for this rest, and for the new day. We ask Thee, O Father, to forgive us wherein we have misused any of Thy great blessings. We repent of all that we have done against Thy will.

Help us remember that Thou hast given us this new day for a purpose, to use wisely in holiness and godliness. May Thy holy name be honored and praised, and our souls be kept by grace unto eternal salvation. May Thy Holy Spirit lead us and Thy guardian angels guide us on our way. O God, we ask this in the name of Thy beloved Son, Jesus Christ, who taught us to pray, Our Father which art in heaven, . . .

A NEW MORNING PRAYER

Dear loving Father, we bow before Thee this morning to thank Thee for another night's rest, for watching over us and keeping us from all harm. We thank Thee for the dawn of a new day, for the opportunities and privileges it brings. We pray that Thou wilt guide and direct our lives today in the use of these benefits to Thy honor and glory.

We confess that we are unworthy of so many blessings. So often we forget the ways in which Thou hast helped us. We become impatient and complain when we cannot have our own way. Forgive us these many faults and sins against Thee. Help us, O Lord, to do better today, and to be more grateful. It is only by Thy boundless mercy that our lives have been spared. Judge us not accoording to our deeds, but grant us mercy through the blood of Jesus Christ, who gave His life for us.

O Heavenly Father, let us be on our guard this day against unclean and lustful thoughts. Keep us from self-righteousness and pride, and from any evil that may secretly enter our hearts. Cleanse us from any fault we do not see. Let our thoughts, our words and deeds, ever be pure, kind, and good. Show us the good in our fellow men, that we may love our neighbors as ourselves. May we be anxious to bear each other's burdens, in Christian love.

We pray, O Lord, for all our fellow Christians, wherever they may be. Especially do we pray for the ministers and teachers who are laboring to make known Thy Word and Thy will in many parts of the earth. Supply their every need, comfort and strengthen them, and protect them from every danger. Give them wisdom and discernment to perform their duties in a way that is pleasing to Thee. Cause us to remember those who labor in Thy vineyard, and to assist them in anything they need.

We pray for all those who are still living in sin, who do not yet know Thee. May they repent and obtain salvation in this time of grace. O Lord, we pray for those who are new in the faith. Help them to grow, and keep them firmly anchored on Jesus Christ, the rock of their salvation. Keep them from falling, and help them to live a victorious life, a true testimony for Thee.

We pray for all those who have strayed from the narrow way, and have fallen again into sin. Oh, that they might see how grievously they have erred, and repent and again find peace for their souls.

We pray, O heavenly Father, for those

who have authority over us, for the rulers and governments of every nation. Lead them according to Thy holy will. Make us worthy of a government which allows us the freedom to serve Thee.

O Lord, we pray for those who are sick, in sorrow or pain, for those who are discouraged. We pray for the widows and the fatherless, for the aged and afflicted, and for those who suffer for Thy name's sake.

Into Thy hands we commit ourselves, our children, parents, brothers and sisters, friends, and all who are dear to us. Protect us this day against all dangers, both to body and soul. Give us a home where love, peace and joy abound. Help us to be patient, kind and good to one another.

May Thy Holy Spirit lead us and the holy angels attend our way. Teach us to pray in spirit and truth, even as Thy Son Jesus Christ has taught us, Our Father which art in heaven, . . .

ANOTHER MORNING PRAYER

O God and Father of all light and comfort, Thy mercies are new every morning and great is Thy faithfulness. We praise and honor Thee for this new day, and that Thou hast kept us safely through another night and given us rest and sleep. Let us now arise by Thy grace and under Thy care, to use the hours of this day in a worthwhile way.

Above all, brighten our pathway with the eternal light, our Lord Jesus Christ, that He may live in us with His grace and knowledge. Keep us growing in the true faith, give us Thy true love in our hearts, strengthen hope, and make us humble to follow in the footsteps of our Lord and Master, Jesus Christ. In all that we do, let a godly fear of evil be before our eyes. Drive from our hearts all wickedness and spiritual blindness.

Keep us free of all superstition and idolatry, of pride and disobedience, of blasphemy and wrath, lest the sun of this day set upon our anger. Protect us from hostility, envy and hatred, uncleanness and iniquity, from dishonesty and greed and every unlawful desire. Awake in us a hunger and thirst for Thy Word and righteousness. Teach us to act according to Thy will, for we are Thy children, and Thy Spirit shall guide us upon paths of righteousness.

We commit ourselves unto Thy keeping. May all our deeds bear friut and bring honor to Thy name. Make us the vessels of Thy grace, and restrain all those who would hinder us.

Shield us from the slanderous tongue and from the darts of liars. Encompass us with Thy grace and keep Thy hand over us at all times, whether we be at home or away, asleep or awake. Keep us from sickness and disease. Bless our food and all that is necessary to our well being, and let us not waste the things which Thou hast given us.

Protect us from wars, famine and pestilence, and from a sudden or unexpected death. Care for our souls as we live here day by day, and give us a peaceful departure from this life that we may look forward with joyous anticipation to the appearing of our Lord and Saviour, Jesus Christ.

O heavenly Father, bless and keep us through Jesus Christ and Thy Holy Spirit, henceforth and forevermore.   Amen.

AN EVENING PRAYER

O Lord God, kind and merciful Father, this day Thou didst again so graciously shed abroad the light of heaven upon our pathway, and gaveth us another opportunity to serve Thee and to grow in godliness.

For these many blessings we are grateful to Thee, O heavenly Father, and would praise and glorify Thy name forever. Forgive us, Lord, where we have sinned against Thee, for we confess with sorrow and regret that we have often through carelessness and neglect transgressed Thy law. Forgive us for the sake of Thy dear Son, Jesus Christ, in whose name we pray. Receive and pardon us in His name that we may be reconciled to Thee, and in Thy peace abide eternally.

We pray Thee, O heavenly Father, keep us this night and for the rest of our lives under the shadow and protection of Thy wings. Shield us from the power of the evil one who is continually trying to deceive us and to destroy our souls.

Grant us a peaceful night's rest according to Thy will. Refresh our bodies, minds and spirits, so we may be found watching and waiting, eagerly looking forward to the glorious reappearing of Thy beloved Son when He comes to claim His own.

O holy and merciful Father, let the light of Thy loving kindness illuminate our pathway, lest the gloom of darkness that engulfs the world should also envelop us and lull us to a spiritual death. Rather, let us arise and walk in a newness of life, all to the honor and glory of Thy holy name, and to our eternal salvation.

We pray, O loving Father, for all Thy children who are in need. Especially do we remember the sick and weak, the sorrowing and troubled, and those who suffer for Thy name's sake. We also pray for our enemies and for those who mistreat us, for they do not realize what they are doing.

We pray that Thou wouldst send faithful workers in Thy harvest, and ministers who preach Thy holy Word according to Thy will. We pray for the government of our land, and for the rulers of all nations and cities. Also, for all sorrowful, oppressed and destitute souls.

Thou knoweth all our needs, dear Father. We pray that Thou wilt give to each one of us what is of greatest service to us. Protect us with Thy great power and watch over us, for we are Thy creation, the work of Thy hands. Prepare us for Thy eternal salvation.

All this we pray in the name of Thy dear son, Jesus Christ, who has taught us to ask in His name, Our Father which art in heaven, . . .

We commit ourselves, dear Father, with all our loved ones into Thy hands. May Thy angels attend us this night and Thy Holy Spirit guide us through the tribulations of this life, to face death with confidence, and arise with joy to enter our eternal home. This we ask in the name of Thy beloved Son, Jesus Christ. Amen.

A SHORT EVENING PRAYER

O merciful heavenly Father, we thank Thee for letting us live through another day. Thou hast given us light and strength to live according to Thy will, but we confess that we have often failed in this, for which we ask Thy forgiveness. We ask that Thou wilt bless us with Thy grace as we lie down to rest, and wilt keep us in the shadow of Thy wings.

Protect us from the cunning wiles of the enemy who goes about day and night, seeking to destroy us. May we enter into this night's rest with grateful hearts, and be ever watchful and ready for the return of Thy beloved Son, Jesus Christ, in whose name we offer this prayer, Our Father which art in heaven, . . .

A GENERAL PRAYER

O Lord my God, Thou who understandeth the need of every human heart, comfort me in my distress. Forgive me where I have sinned, for my mistakes are many in word and in deed.

O Lord, teach me the truth in Thy holy Word. Be merciful and do not charge my sins to my account. Call me not to judgement, but as an affectionate father has mercy on his children, so have Thou mercy upon me.

In deep sincerity I pray Thee, teach me the true faith, hope and love, which lead to sanctification and eternal salvation. Oh, loving Father, give me strength in my weakness, and health instead of sickness, both in body and soul. Put on me the armor of Thy spiritual power that I may be able to withstand the fiery darts of the enemy, who fights against the truth. Give me the shield of true faith to win the victory over all that would hinder me from attaining Thy love and righteousness.

O Thou holy Father in heaven, Thou didst hear the prayers of Elijah and the Apostle Paul, hear also my prayer and deliver me from evil. Thou didst save Noah in the ark, save Thou me through the Ark of the New Testament that my name may be found written in the Book of Life.

O righteous Father, feed me with the Living Bread which is Thy divine Word, and give me to drink from the fountain of living waters, Thy Holy Spirit. Keep Thy holy eyes upon me, that I may turn from evil.

Protect me from wars and violence, and

from all temptations that would deceive me or separate me from Thy love and righteousness. Grant that the intercession of Thy Son Jesus Christ and the prayers of the saints for me may not be in vain.

O heavenly Father, be merciful to me and protect me from the gross sins of adultery, fornication, impurity, lasciviousness, idolatry, witchcraft, malice, quarreling, jealousy, anger, strife, dissension, revelling, drunkenness and such like, which would separate me from Thy great love.

Deliver me, O Father, from the bondage of these sins. Cleanse me and wash me in the waters of Thy living Word, so that I may at all times pray in truth and in Spirit, Our Father which art in heaven, . . .

A PRAYER FOR CHRISTIAN VIRTUE

In all sincerity we pray, O loving Father, anchor Thou us firmly on the solid foundation of Thy Word, and draw us nearer to Thee. Give us willing hearts to faithfully serve Thee and keep Thy commandments. Let ours be the gift of genuine faith, with hope and love, and make us loyal and true to Thee. Yea, give us a true knowledge of Jesus Christ through Thy Holy Word and Spirit that we may gladly do Thy will.

Give us a hate and abhorrence of all evil so that we will love only what Thou loveth and hate what Thou hateth. Be our guide on our journey through life and keep Thy protecting hand over us at all times that we may walk in the paths of peace. Move us to love and serve Thee as Thy children and true servants until our life here is ended.

Present us understanding and wisdom in both spiritual and material things, and give us a holy desire and will to do our duty according to the talents Thou hast given us. Impart to all mankind the gift of Thy grace and goodness, as Thou seest fit. Supply the needs of each of us and comfort those of us who are in sorrow and afflicted in body and spirit. This we pray, O heavenly Father, in the name of Thy Son Jesus Christ. Amen.

FOR REMISSION OF SINS

We pray, gracious Father, have mercy on us in these last perilous times. Forgive us all our sins and shortcomings, whether they be done openly or in secret, knowingly or unknowingly. Give us true repentance for anything we have done against Thy will, by word or by deed. Humbly we pray, be merciful toward us, O Father, for Jesus' sake. Amen.

A PRAYER FOR GOD'S BLESSINGS

Eternal Father, Thou knoweth our sin and unworthiness. Without Thee we can do nothing. By nature we are evil, vain, and defiled, yea, poor miserable sinful creatures and worms of the dust.

O heavenly Father, give us the grace to call to Thee as to a loving Father, give us help and comfort in the hour of need, accept our prayer of praise and thanksgiving, and continue to favor us with showers of blessings from Thy throne on high.

Increase our faith and cleanse our hearts so we can truly pray as Thy Son Jesus has taught us, Our Father which art in heaven, . . .

A PRAYER FOR THE BRETHREN

We pray, O heavenly Father, for all our brethren and sisters in the faith wherever they may be, even unto the ends of the earth, whether they be assembled or scattered, in sorrow or sickness, in bonds or in prison for Thy name's sake, or in any other way enduring trials and sufferings. Comfort them with Thy great love and keep them with Thy Holy Spirit in Thy Word and will. May they abide in Thy love and not depart from the way of righteousness, neither to the right nor to the left, but remain faithful unto the end of their lives.

In Jesus' holy name. Amen.

A PRAYER FOR THE GOVERNMENTS

We also pray, dear Father, for all mankind throughout the world, for all those for which it is Thy will for us to pray. We pray for the governments and rulers of the nations, especially of those lands where Thy children are. Do not permit them to shed innocent blood, but inspire them to rule according to Thy will as Thou intended for them to do. May they at all times promote the good and discourage and repress the evil, so that we who fear Thy name may lead quiet and peaceful lives here on earth. Amen.

A PRAYER FOR FAITHFUL WORKERS

O Lord of the harvest, truly the harvest is great but the laborers are few. Awaken among us, O Lord, faithful teachers, fervent workers who will plant the seeds of truth throughout the world. Give us such men who are godly-minded, have found grace in Thine eyes, and are able to work according to Thy will. May they preach Thy Word in the power of the Spirit in meekness and sincerity, to the honor and glory of Thy name.

O heavenly Father, provide a way for Thy Word to grow and increase and be spread abroad as far as possible, so that we may all be taught and become established in the faith. All those who hunger and thirst after Thy righteousness, Thy kingdom, Thy love, and Thy Holy Word and Gospel, heavenly Father, feed Thou with the bread and water of life.

We pray for Thy messengers and servants who are sent forth to preach Thy holy Word and to proclaim Thy great truths. Endow them with humility, divine wisdom, a good report and a pious life that by word and example they may preach the good news according to Thy will and pleasure.

We pray that Thy ministry may be continued through the laying on of holy hands, and be directed to our great spiritual needs, to the honor and glory of Thy holy name, and the welfare of our soul and body, in time and eternity.

In Jesus' name.   Amen.

PRAYER FOR A PURE HEART

O Thou holy and noble Lord Jesus, Thou art the lover of purity and the crown of all virtue. I confess that the nature of my heart is carnal, and my body and soul have often been stained by impure thoughts, words, and deeds. O merciful Father, forgive my iniquity and withhold from me the punishment which Thou hast promised the disobedient.

If the pure in heart shall see God, then those who are impure will understandably never see His face. Therefore, create in me a clean heart, O God, and renew a right spirit within me. Cast me not away from Thy presence, and take not Thy Holy Spirit from me. I know that without Thy help I can not live a chaste and modest life, so I humbly beseech Thee, sanctify and consecrate my life through the Holy Spirit unto true repentance. Through the New Birth, strengthen me to subdue my carnal nature and not let it rule my body and soul. For if the unclean spirit again enters this house it will be worse with me than beforehand. Extinguish the flames of lasciviousness within me, and clothe me with modesty.

O noble Bridegroom of my soul, subdue my heart with Thy great love, make me minded even as Thou art, fill my soul with noble and pure thoughts. Make me a part of Thy body and a vessel of honor, not a servant of Satan and a vessel of dishonor.

I need Thy grace to wisely use the talents Thou hast given me, to be a vessel of Thy mercy. With discipline and purity, let me be

separate from deceiving spirits and all unrighteousness, lest I lose my inheritance in the
New Jerusalem. Draw me to Thee, that I may
be one spirit, one mind, and one body with
Thee, even as Thou hast washed me from my
sins and through baptism set me apart to be
a temple of Thy Holy Spirit. Oh, teach me
that my body is the dwelling place of Thy
Spirit, and let me not defile it. Keep me from
sinning against my own body.

O noble heavenly Bridegroom, Thou abid-
eth where grow roses of purity; let me feed
upon the knowledge of Thy pure love, and
be cleansed from all evil thoughts. Come and
live within me with Thy Holy Spirit, and may
the holy angels be with me ever.   Amen.

IN PRAISE OF GOD'S GRACE

O heavenly Father, we praise and thank
Thee for Thy unspeakable grace and for Thy
immeasurable love, which Thou hast bestowed
upon us through Jesus Christ, our Lord and
Saviour. Thou hast bought us, O Lord, and
redeemed us by Thy precious atonement upon
the cross. Thou hast permitted Thy blood to
be shed and Thy body to be broken as a holy
and perfect sacrifice for our sins.

We could not have been saved except for
Thy bitter suffering and death so willingly
endured for our sakes.

Therefore, we hope and believe that Thou wilt through Thy grace and mercy lead us forth on that great Resurrection morning into Thy eternal Kingdom. O Heavenly Father and Thy Son Jesus Christ and the Holy Spirit, three-fold but one, may Thy holy name be praised, honored, and exalted now and in all eternity. Amen.

A PRAYER OF DISCIPLESHIP

Most gracious and beloved Lord, Jesus Christ, meek and lowly and patient Saviour! What a beautiful and perfect example of a holy life Thou hast given us! Thou art the pure and lustrous mirror of virtue, the perfect pattern of holiness, the standard of piety and the yardstick of righteousness. Oh, the contrast between our sinful lives and Thy holy one! We would live in Thee as regenerated creatures, but so often our sinful nature asserts itself in word and deed.

O Thou gentle, patient, longsuffering Lord! Forgive us all our sins, our shortcomings, our mistakes. Look not upon our uncleanness, and do not cast us away as hopeless. Sift from our hearts every trace of pride, which is of the devil, and plant in us the seeds of humility as the root and foundation of virtue.

Purge from us all resentment and revenge, and fill us with meekness so precious in Thy sight. O Thou highest embodiment of virtue, adorn our hearts with the true faith, with a burning love, a living hope, and a child-like reverence. Thou art our sole trust, our faith and hope, our honor and splendor. Thy life was nothing but love, meekness, and humility. Make us partakers of Thy divine nature, so that Thy virtuous life may be reflected in our lives. Cause us to be one spirit, one body and soul with Thee. Bless us with true knowledge and grace to follow Thy footsteps. If Thou art our light, so shine in us; if Thou art our life, so live in us; if Thou art our joy, fill us with rejoicing; if we are temples of Thy Spirit, take full possession of us and make us holy in body, soul, and spirit. O Eternal Way, lead us; Eternal Truth, teach us; Eternal Life, revive us. Let not the evil one fulfil in us his wickedness, deceit, pride, greed, anger and uncleanness, but deliver us from his snares.

Renew us daily in body, spirit and soul until we are made perfect in Thee. Let us die to the world, that we may live; let us arise to go with Thee to heaven; let us be crucified with Thee so we may enter into Thy eternal glory. Amen.

A PRAYER FOR THE SUPPORT AND COMFORT OF THE HOLY SPIRIT

We, Thy forsaken and afflicted children, are surrounded by sorrow, anxiety and many dangers because of our sins. In prayer we call upon Thee today, O Holy Spirit of our Heavenly Father and our Lord Jesus Christ. Come to us and cast the bright rays of Thy divine light into our sin-sick hearts. May we see in Thy light the eternal light and true knowledge of our Lord Jesus Christ.

Come, Thou Father of afflicted ones! O generous Giver of all blessings. Come, O Cleanser of impure hearts and perform Thy work in us. Sanctify our hearts, even as Thou hast been sent out by the Father to comfort those who long for Thee. Support us with Thy power in all our time of need and temptation. Help us to overcome our own sinful nature, as well as the world and the evil spirits. Cleanse our hearts from all wickedness and impurity, and control our eyes and our tongue so that our conversation, our deeds and thoughts, may be pleasing to Thee. Help us to be moderate and reasonable in all things as true children of God.

O beloved Comforter of despondent hearts, O worthy Guest of faithful souls, O sweet Refresher and sole Sustainer in our infirmities, draw near and make Thy abode in us forever.

Strengthen us when we are fainthearted, purify that which is filthy, heal that which is wounded, make straight that which is twisted, renew our spirit when we are unconcerned, reclaim and bring back to the right path that which is astray and lost.

Thou holiest Light, let the brightness of Thy grace shine deep into the hearts of Thy faithful ones, who this day commit anew their souls to Thy keeping. We are truly sorry that we have grieved Thee or hindered Thy work within us.

Thou hast taught us that we are nothing of ourselves. Without Thy help, power and influence, we can not accomplish that which is good and acceptable to Thee. We admit and confess our sins,—yes, everything wherein we have opposed Thy teachings, knowingly or unknowingly, in thoughts or intentions, in word or deed. We are poor, wretched and helpless without Thee, and our only hope is that Jesus Christ the Son of God has shown compassion toward us. For this we bring praise and thanks. We are confident He will never leave us, but will intercede for us before our Heavenly Father.

O Holy Spirit, as Thou art the Spirit of the Lord Jesus Christ, so bless us with loyalty, love and goodness. Let us be filled with Thy great power, and give the weak in faith who have newly yielded themselves to Thee, a regenerated heart.

Give us Thy seven holy gifts, the spirit of wisdom and understanding, the spirit of counsel and might, the spirit of knowledge and the fear of the Lord and all godliness. Share with us poor forsaken ones these gracious gifts of Thy unspeakable love and goodness. Yes, for His sake who has redeemed us with His precious blood.

O God , Holy Spirit, come from above without delay. Look not upon our many shortcomings, for we long to be rid of them all. Cleanse us more and more each day, and have mercy on us.

Claim our hearts as Thine own and fill them with heavenly comfort and joy, so that we may be cheerful and satisfied under all circumstances. As children of God, help us to overcome the world. Praise be to Thee, O Holy Spirit and God the Father and the Son, in eternity.   Amen.

A PRAYER FOR CHRISTIAN VIRTUES

O heavenly Father, from whom all good and perfect blessings flow; O Father of light, who worketh in us both to will and to do according to Thy good pleasure; O Lord Jesus Christ, the Author and Finisher of our faith; and, O Holy Spirit, who bringeth about all things according to Thy will, we pray that Thou wilt finish Thy work begun in us, even unto the day of our Lord Jesus Christ, that we may grow and increase in knowledge and maturity. Show us what is the best for us, and keep us pure and blameless, filled with the fruits of the Spirit through Jesus Christ, to the honor of God.

O God, Thou hast given us heavenly treasures in earthen vessels, but the devil, the world and our own flesh and blood trouble us and war against the soul. Help us to fight the good fight of faith and gain the victory, offering our bodies as a living sacrifice, holy and acceptable unto Thee. May we be completely transformed through the renewing of the mind, to prove what is that good, and acceptable, and perfect will of God.

Give us, O Lord Jesus, power according to the abundance of Thy grace to be strong in faith, that Thy true love may be implanted in our hearts. Help us to grasp the breadth and length, the height and depth of the unsearchable riches of Christ, and to know that to be filled with the love of Christ is better than all knowledge.

O loving heavenly Father, it is Thy will that none should be lost whom Thou hast given to Thy dear Son, so sustain us in the faith, anchor us in Thy love, and strengthen our hope.

O holy Trinity, come and abide in us, possess and fill us with Thy grace, and in eternity with Thy eternal glory. Give ear to our prayers and send us Thy Holy Spirit, who may through Thy Word sanctify, teach, and strengthen us and preserve us unto eternal life.

Remember, Lord, Thy mercy and goodness which Thou hast shown mankind from the beginning of the world. Do not think of the sins and mistakes of our youthful years but remember us according to Thy mercy and compassion.

O Lord Jesus, give us true repentance and remorse for our sins, the godly sorrow that worketh repentance to salvation. Impart to us a spirit of love, of meekness, of humility, of reverence, of grace, of prayer, and the fear of the Lord, so that we may with all the saints inherit the Kingdom and gain eternal life.

O God, light our path with Thy Holy Spirit and keep our hearts from being led astray by the world, the lust of the eyes, the lust of the flesh, and the pride of life. Let us ever adore Thee and praise Thy name, never blaspheme or deny Thee in time of persecution, but confess Thy name even under penalty of death.

May Thy kingdom abide in us forever more, and the devil's kingdom be utterly destroyed. Keep us from error and dishonesty, ignorance and a darkened heart. Multiply in us righteousness, peace and love in the Holy Spirit, and the Peace of God which passes all understanding preserve our hearts and thoughts in Jesus Christ, our Lord.

O God, help us to gladly do Thy will and to crucify our own selfish desires. And when the hour of our departure comes, grant that the eternal name of Jesus may be our last word and prayer, and that we may peacefully fall asleep in Him and joyously arise in the resurrection of the saints, through Jesus Christ. Amen.

A TRAVELER'S PRAYER

O heavenly Father, merciful and faithful God, we thank Thee heartily that Thou hast so kindly watched over us, and hath favored us with many blessings in body and soul. We are weak and sinful, but we pray that Thou wilt forgive all our misdeeds for Christ's sake.

Cleanse and renew us more and more through the power of the Holy Spirit, that we can daily grow in grace and serve Thee in holiness and righteousness.

O heavenly Father, be with us, lead and direct us at all times. Protect us from thieves and murderers, disease and all misfortunes. Give us, O Lord, food and clothing, and lead us on the path we ought to go. Keep us in Thy will and let Thy blessing rest upon all our undertakings, to Thy honor and the edification of all Thy children. Keep us and all our loved ones safely, and grant that we may again meet each other with peace and joy. Especially protect us from the devices and wickedness of Satan and his evil ones.

Strengthen us in the true saving faith; give us repentance, patience, and hope to finish the course of our days with a good conscience and enter the heavenly Fatherland. To Thee, O Lord, we commit our whole lives, our going out and our coming in, from now unto all eternity. Amen. Our Father which art in heaven . . .

A PRAYER OF PARENTS FOR THEIR CHILDREN

Dear God and Father, Creator and Guardian of all living beings, give us the grace to bring up our children in the nurture and admonition of the Lord. Help us to be an example of all virtue. Give our children grace and the gifts of the Spirit so they will profit from the admonitions we give them. Kindle in them the true fear of God, which is the beginning of all wisdom. Fill them with the desire to do Thy will and to claim Thy promises.

Favor them with true knowledge and keep them from all idolatry and false teachings. May they learn to know the true faith and to practice all godly virtues, remaining steadfast unto the end. Give them a faithful and obedient mind, with true wisdom and understanding. Let them increase in wisdom and stature, and in favor with God and man.

Implant in their hearts a fervent love for Thy holy Word. May they be attentive to prayer and devotions, respectful toward the ministers and toward everyone, honest and upright in all their doings. Help them to show love and forbearance to all. Protect them from the evil influence of this world, so they will not be led astray by evil companions.

May they never indulge in evil, nor give offense to others. Be a shield unto them in all kinds of danger lest they be overtaken by a violent or untimely death.

Let Thy church here on earth be preserved and enlarged by us, our children and descendants. Finally, may we all meet in the celestial heavens, with the innumerable multitudes, with palm leaves in our hands, to sing the new song with joy and praise to Thee forever. This we pray in Jesus' name.   Amen.

A PRAYER TO PRECEDE THE SERMON

O Lord, Almighty God, holy and heavenly Father, Thou art our Creator and Saviour, our strength and stay. Not only doth Thou so bountifully supply our material needs, but feedeth our souls with the true bread from heaven, unto eternal life.

But we, Thy poor children, do not live by bread alone, but by every word that proceedeth out of Thy mouth, according to the words of Thy beloved Son, Jesus Christ, in whose name we are here assembled to preach, hear, and understand Thy holy Word and will.

We thank Thee, O God, from the depth of our hearts, that Thou hast kindled within us this ardor, love, and zeal to Thy work. Thou hast brought us thus together in one accord, but we confess, O heavenly Father, that we are by nature unworthy, unable, and unqualified to preach Thy Holy Word, much less to heed and obey it, without the help, presence, and grace of Thy Holy Spirit. Therefore, we pray Thee, dear Father, that Thou wouldest at this time look upon us with Thy merciful eyes and fulfill in us the promise of Thy dear Son.

O Christ, be present in this assembly, we pray, with the power and grace of Thy Holy Spirit. Make Thy servant worthy to preach Thy Holy Word boldly and with discernment, and bestow Thy blessings upon his labors. Give us open and obedient hearts, cleansed from all idle thoughts and cares of this world, so that we may hear and understand and obey Thy Holy Word.

O Lord, to the honor and praise of Thy holy, exalted, and glorious name, may many be led and shown the eternal plan of salvation. This we pray in the name of Thy dear Son, Jesus Christ, our Lord and Saviour, who has taught us to pray earnestly, Our Father which art in heaven, . . .

A PRAYER TO FOLLOW THE SERMON

O Thou merciful and gracious God, dear heavenly Father, Thou dost show us, Thy poor children, overflowing kindness and favor. Not only hast Thou given us the desire and zeal to assemble ourselves here, but Thou hast also, as so many times before, let us

hear the preaching of Thy word and the pro-
claiming of Thy will. For these great favors,
Lord, we praise and thank Thee from the
depths of our hearts.

We freely confess our guilt, O Lord, for
we have so many times been admonished and
have heard Thy warnings, yet have not shown
true obedience. Forgive us this for the sake
of Thy beloved Son, Jesus Christ.

We entreat Thee, O loving Father, to
bless the Word which we have heard and received into our hearts, that it may bring forth
much fruit for the life to come. Help us not
only to repent and be born again and changed
to Thy image, but that we may also grow to
maturity in Christ, and in grace and knowledge of the true faith.

Set Thy Word as a mirror before our
hearts, that we may be washed in the living
waters and bring forth fruits of righteousness. Heal and renew our sin-sick souls by
Thy sharp and powerful Word, which is able
to separate soul and spirit, joint and marrow,
that we may be no longer carnal-minded but
spiritual. Make us anxious to do good, but in
meekness and humility. Let us taste of Thy
grace and Thy heavenly kingdom, and seek
our happiness there. Help us to withstand
the temptations of the evil one and to have
victory at all times.

We pray, O heavenly Father, for all our needs in the name of Thy beloved Son, our Lord Jesus Christ, who has taught us to fervently pray, Our Father which art in heaven, . . .

A PRAYER AT BAPTISM

O Almighty God, merciful, loving Father, Thou didst know from the beginning that man would not remain innocent, but would come to the fall and bring condemnation upon himself. And because Thou didst love Thy creation, Thou hast prepared a way of escape and did not spare Thine only begotten Son, but sent Him for our sake so that all who believe in Him should not perish but have everlasting life. Thou hast offered Thy love and grace through Thy Holy Gospel, and commanded that all who believe should be baptized in the name of Jesus.

By Thy grace and command, it is the heartfelt desire of these souls before us to thus be baptized. They wait with hearts bowed before Thee, prepared to fulfill Thy holy will and the command of Thy Son.

Look down from above, we pray Thee, upon these feeble creatures, and give them power to be victorious over sin, the world, the devil and hell, worthy to receive heavenly crowns. Remove from their hearts all love of this world, that they may be clean and beautiful and serve only Christ as their Bridegroom. Let them forsake the devil's kingdom of sin and corruption, and become heirs in Thy heavenly kingdom of righteousness. In the covenant which they are now making with Thee, give them a good conscience of the forgiveness of their sins and a joyful hope unto eternal life.

O heavenly Father, receive them in Thy grace, forgive all their sins, and set them apart as Thy children and heirs of Thy heavenly promises.

O Christ, Thou Son of God, impart to them the merits of Thy grace and excellence, that they may be accounted worthy and righteous. Wash them in Thy blood and accept them as brothers and sisters and heirs of Thy heavenly kingdom.

O generous Holy Spirit, endow them with Thy gifts, anchor them in the faith, cause them to feel the need of prayer, renew their spirit to subdue the flesh and obey Thy commands. Sustain and strengthen their faith to overcome all opposition. May this all be to Thy honor and glory, and to the salvation of their souls. For this cause we pray in unity of spirit, Our Father which art in heaven, . . .

In Thy name, O God, this work is begun; complete it through Thy grace and power. This we pray through Thy Son, Jesus Christ. Amen.

A GENERAL PRAYER
(For Fast and Prayer Days)

O Lord, our God, teach us to pray on this day of prayer and fasting. Thou art a Spirit, and would have us pray in spirit and in truth. Too often we have appeared before Thee with empty words; we have drawn near to Thee with our lips while our hearts were far away. Be gracious to us and forgive us, for Thou knoweth, O Lord, how wretched and unworthy we are to converse with such a holy God. Give us Thy Spirit to draw near to Thee in the name of Jesus, and to bring to Thee our prayers.

We pray for all men, for the rulers and governments, that we may live a quiet and peaceful life in all godliness and honesty. Thou wouldst have all men to be saved and to come to the knowledge of the truth.

Be merciful to the sick and the suffering, and comfort all sorrowful and discouraged souls with Thy Holy Spirit, and show them the

Way of Life. We pray, O God, that Thou wilt consider us and be merciful to Thy people. Be Thou our God and let us be Thy people.

Give our government the spirit of wisdom and justice. Let all those who exercise authority remember that they have over them a God in heaven. Let not those who rule be the servants of sin and corruption, to pervert the power which Thou hast delegated unto them. May they through their offices be a blessing to the nation. May all citizens respect and obey the laws, that right and good may be promoted. Let us live peaceably with each other, respecting one another and serving God faithfully and in love.

Protect us from well-deserved pestilence, war and famine, from fire or other misfortune. Bless the fruits of the earth that they may bring forth in abundance what is needful to man.

We entreat Thee, O God, have mercy upon Thy church here on earth. Help the ministers and messengers who carry forth Thy Word; open their mouths to proclaim Thy wondrous grace. May they be true witnesses and watchers on the walls of Zion, shepherds after Thine own heart, dependable and trustworthy servants in Thy work. Let them not seek their own, but Thy honor, as true spiritual pilgrims. Bless their ministry and help them fulfill their duties with joy. May they always possess the sincere loyalty, the respect and confidence of all the members of the church for whom they labor, and over whose souls they watch. Prevent all disagreements in life and doctrine, and all divisions. Be reconciled to Thy sheep and gather them together in one faith and hope under the Bishop of our souls, the praiseworthy Captain and Head of Thy church, Jesus Christ.

We also pray for our schools and the teachers. Let Thy Spirit be upon the teachers, and help the children to become wise, not merely for this life but for eternity. Give our youth a concern to learn what is needful for their everlasting peace. Implant in our young men and women Thy holy fear, to live blamelessly according to Thy Word, as members of Thy church.

Bless in particular each household and let love and peace reign in every family. Vanquish the spirit of strife and division which would separate the hearts from each other.

Give the parents wisdom and tact to nurture their children, and to all children, give obedience and love. Let all brothers and sisters live peaceably with each other. Give those who must use authority, righteousness, patience, and friendliness| Help all servants to do their duties loyally without complaining. Be merciful to all people in all circumstances; let none be put to shame who trusts in Thee, the Living God.

Dear heavenly Father, we commit ourselves unto Thy care, with the assurance that all things will work together for the good of each one of us. To Thy holy name be all honor, praise, and gratitude, now and in eternity. Amen.

A PRAYER AT HOLY COMMUNION

O Lord, almighty God and merciful, loving Father, we are assembled at this time to commemorate the broken body and the shed blood of Thy dear Son, Jesus Christ. O heavenly Father, we pray that Thou would prepare our hearts for this ceremony, and make us worthy as spiritual pilgrims to partake of these sacred emblems. Help us to understand the mystery of this sacrament that we may observe it to Thy honor and the welfare of our souls.

We freely confess all our sins, our weaknesses and shortcomings, and come to Thee naked, without any righteousness of our own. We seek only the righteousness of Christ which he hath obtained for us through His bitter death and suffering on the cross. O Lord, may our hungry souls receive nourishment through the grace and gift of Thy Holy Spirit, to partake of the emblems of His body and blood. May Christ abide in us and we in Him, that His suffering on our account be not in vain, but that we may be comforted and receive assurance in our hearts through the breaking of this bread.

Make us worthy to claim Thy promises. For Thou art a merciful and watchful God who careth for us at all times.

We thank Thee from the depth of our hearts for the consolation and help Thou giveth. We pray that Thou would keep us the remaining years of our lives in faith, in love and patience, and help us to willingly carry the cross Thou giveth us. Let us serve Thee the whole of our lives in temperance, righteousness, and a godly fear, growing in grace and virtue, to the honor of Thy holy name. Amen. Our Father which art in heaven, . . .

THANKS FOR THE BREAD

O Lord, Almighty God, loving heavenly Father, because Thou loved us so greatly Thou hast given Thy dear Son, Jesus Christ, to redeem us from eternal death. Feed our hungry souls with Thy heavenly bread unto eternal life. We praise and thank Thee for Thy grace that called us poor mortals to this blessed communion. To Thy Son, Jesus Christ, our Redeemer, be all praise and honor and glory in eternity.   Amen.

THANKS FOR RECEIVING THE CUP

O Lord, Almighty God, loving heavenly Father, Thou hast led us out from sin by the hand of Thy Son, Jesus Christ, the one great Shepherd of Thy sheep, who shed His blood on Calvary as an everlasting atonement for our sins. Through grace Thou hast called us to this blessed communion, for which we praise and thank Thee forever, in the name of Thy Son, Jesus Christ.   Amen.

A WEDDING PRAYER

O Lord, almighty merciful Father, in Thy eternal wisdom Thou hast decreed that it is not good for man, created in Thy image, to be alone. Therefore, Thou gavest him a helpmeet, a wife taken from his side, that the human race might be increased and uncleanness prevented.

Thou hast given us Thy sacred marriage laws, and reaffirmed them by Thy dear Son,

Jesus Christ. To begin this union according to Thy will, these two now stand before Thee, O God; have mercy on them and bless them. Let their hearts and minds be stayed on Thee, seeking Thy honor and their souls' salvation. May this marriage begin and be fulfilled in a way that is fitting to Thy children. Help them to withstand the temptations of the evil one, and comfort them in all tribulations and sufferings.

This we pray in their behalf, O loving Father, in the name of Thy beloved Son, Jesus Christ, who has taught us to pray in time of need, Our Father which art in heaven, . . .

COMFORT FOR A SICK PERSON

O Lord, merciful, holy and righteous God, I confess to Thee that my countless sins have provoked Thy righteous wrath. Thou art just and all Thy judgements are true. O how sincerely I regret that I have so often grieved Thee, and have been ungrateful for Thy manifold blessings. O Lord, be not angry and do not remember the sins of my youth and my transgressions, but remember me according to Thy goodness and mercy.

O Lord, it is indeed a righteous judgement with which Thou hast afflicted me, for

I have sinned against Thee. But I turn in faith to the only mercy seat, my Lord Jesus Christ, and with bowed heart pray for mercy.

O Lord, let me obtain grace and mercy; have compassion and remove this burden from me.

O Lord, my sins have corrupted me and my iniquity troubles me. Thou canst heal all by merely speaking one word; forgive me and heal me from this sickness. With believing eyes I look upon the crucified Christ; restore my soul.

This vain body of mine is contaminated by sin and corruption. That is why it is subject to suffering and pain. Be merciful to me, a poor Lazarus lying at Thy door, filled with disease and agony, and desiring to be fed with the bread of Thy grace.

O Loving Father, consider Thy beloved Son who has borne my infirmities and was wounded for my sins. Thou hast, O loving Father, delight in life. Thou art my light and strength, in whom I trust. Do not let me be overcome by my afflictions. Protect me by Thy might and keep me under the shadow of Thy wings. Put Thy seal upon me with the blood of Jesus Christ, the spotless Lamb of God, so that the destroying angel will pass over.

Strengthen me, O Lord, by Thy Spirit and power, and give me a firm, immovable faith. Let me say to Thee: My God, my assurance, in whom I trust. Let me take refuge in Thy wisdom and not be terrified by this infirmity. Send Thy angel to guard me wherever I go.

O Lord, help me, for I long for Thy presence; I acknowledge Thy name and call upon Thee. Hear me, therefore, in this time of need and deliver me by the might of Thy hand. Fill me with Thy eternal grace, through Jesus Christ, our Saviour. Amen.

A FUNERAL PRAYER

O Lord God, merciful loving heavenly Father, we thank Thee that Thou hast created us, not only for this life, but by Thy immeasurable grace hast chosen us from eternity to everlasting life. By Thy Son, Jesus Christ, Thou hast prepared the way for our salvation. We have the living hope and assurance that if we live according to Thy Word we shall inherit the heavenly Jerusalem, in fullness of peace and joy at Thy right hand forevermore.

O loving Father, we thank Thee for all the blessings which Thou hast bestowed upon this departed one, especially that Thou hast now redeemed him (her) from this wicked world, and brought his (her) sorrows to an end, and as we trust, have taken his (her) soul home to Thee.

O Lord, we pray that Thou wilt give each of us eternal life and a joyful resurrection on the Judgement Day. As it is appointed unto men once to die and after this the Judgement, so teach us to number our days that we may apply our hearts unto wisdom. Let us fear Thee, O Lord, and dedicate these few days of our life to Thy service, lest we be found unprepared.

Increase in us the true faith, O Lord, so that we may have the blessed assurance of Thy promises in life as well as in death. Help us to devote our days to holiness, humility, love and charity.

Keep us free from the confusion and love of this world and all that belongs to it and is contrary to the teachings of Thy Word, such as pride, impatience, and anger.

Strengthen us through the power of the Holy Spirit to resist the devil, the world, and our own sinful nature. Help us overcome and obtain the victory over them.

Yes, give us the grace to be prepared

each day, and even each hour, to depart in peace and to enter into the heavenly joys.

Comfort every sick and sorrowing person; be merciful to them all and let them understand that their sufferings are for their own good.

Comfort especially those whose hearts have been saddened by the passing of this loved one. Let them draw nigh to Thee and their hearts be comforted by Thy many blessings.

O Lord, Thou art our God and Creator, and hast given us the breath of life. Direct and order every portion of our lives according to Thy holy purposes. Our every thought and action we commit into Thy hands; guide us according to Thy holy will and pleasure.

But, O God, as the earth is barren without the blessings of Thy rain and dew, so are we likewise barren and unfruitful without the gift of Thy grace, and must wilt and perish. Therefore we pray that Thou wouldst favor us with heavenly dew and showers of blessings so that the field of our hearts may be brought to the full measure of fruitfulness. This we pray in the name of Thy blessed Son, Jesus Christ, our Redeemer.

O holy Father, we pray for our children, and for all children everywhere for whom you would have us pray. Give them wisdom and knowledge to understand Thy ways and Thy Word. Draw them to Thyself with Thy everlasting mercies and eternal truth. Thou art the eternal light, and they are living in this sin-darkened world, so lead them onward in the light of Thy eternal wisdom, favor them with Thy Holy Spirit, protect them from all idolatry and false teachings. Implant in their hearts the only true faith in our Lord and Saviour, Jesus Christ.

O Lord, send forth Thy holy angels to protect them on the journey. Let them be victorious over the devil, the world, and their own flesh and blood.

We pray, O heavenly Father, let not the number of unrighteous ones be increased by us or our children. But give us grace to train up our children in the nurture and admonition of the Lord and in all Christian virtues. May we never punish them in wrath but at all times be a good example in life and teachings, so that they may benefit and the number of the righteous be increased thereby.

We pray Thee, O loving Father, for widows and orphans and for all who are in affliction and sorrow. Give them the needed patience to remain steadfast and faithful unto the end.

O Lord, have mercy on all our enemies and all those who hate Thee and Thy children, and are living unconcerned of their salvation. Show them how greatly they have sinned against Thee so they may become alarmed and do true works of repentance.

And finally, O Lord, when our dying hour approaches, strengthen us with the power of Thy Spirit to finish the good fight of faith and win the crown of life awaiting those who look forward to the return of Thy Son.

Into Thy hands, O Lord, we commit our souls. Thou hast redeemed us through Jesus Christ.   Amen.

Rules of a Godly Life
Part I

(Translated from
the German "Regeln eines Gott-
seligen Lebens," as found in the
First Part of "Geistliches Lust-
Gartlein Frommer Seelen.")

Beloved friend, if you desire to live
a holy and God-pleasing life, and to
inherit a home in heaven after this life,
then you must bring ALL of your life,
all your thoughts, words, and actions
into subjection to the teachings of the
Bible, as God has commanded. Deut. 5:
32, 33. This is your only Rulebook of
Faith. King David wrote, "I thought on
my ways, and turned my feet unto thy
testimonies" (Ps. 119:59), as much as
to say — "I regard and examine all my
thoughts, words, and deeds, to see if
they are according to thy commands;
so that, perchance, if I have erred or
wandered from some truth, I may return to the right."

First of all, let us consider our THOUGHTS. Take the following rules seriously to heart:

1. Awake in the morning with your thoughts turned to God. Think, this might be your last day of life. And when you go to bed at night, pause a moment to realize that it is unknown to you whether you will awake again on this earth, or whether your next awakening may be at the resurrection. For this reason, we can see that it is expedient to pray daily; in the morning and again at evening, come before God upon your knees, thanking Him for continued care, confessing your sins and shortcomings, and praying for forgiveness.

2. Keep free from wicked, idle, or unclean thoughts. Prov. 4.23. For as your thoughts are so is your speech, your conduct, and your entire way of life.

3. Think often on the four last things: on death — there is nothing of which we are more sure; on the Judgment

Day — there is nothing more terrible; on hell — there is nothing more unbearable; and on heaven — there is nothing more joyful. He who thinks on these things will shun much sin and will be diligent in the way of salvation.

4. On the Sabbath especially take note of the wonderful works of God; of the creation and governing of the world, and of our Redemption. Make the Sabbath a day of prayer, of listening to and studying sermons; make it a day of holy thoughts and holy conversation. In this way you can keep the Sabbath holy, as is so often commanded in God's Word. If one does not keep the Sabbath holy it is certain that he will also take into contempt all the other commandments of God.

5. In everything you do, ponder well before you start what the outcome may be. Think, would you be willing to be found doing what you plan to do should you be called that hour by death, to appear before God? Never allow your-

self to become involved in anything which destroys your hope and assurance of salvation. Live each day as if it were your last.

6. If anyone wrongs you, exercise a forgiving spirit and patiently dismiss the matter. For if you take the wrong to heart and become angry, you hurt no one but yourself and only do what your enemy wants you to do. If, however, you patiently forgive him, God will in His own good time judge the evildoer and bring your innocence to light.

7. Beware especially of an uncontented and rebellious spirit. Actually it is through the will and grace of God that you suffer and are troubled. God has blessed you with unnumbered gifts to supply your needs, and likewise for your own good has meted out of trouble and pain that you may remain humble. In the midst of trouble remember that you through your sinfulness deserve much greater punishment.

8. If other people praise you, humble yourself. But do not praise yourself or boast, for that is the way of fools who seek vain praise. Be honest in all your dealings and this will be enough reward; then others will praise you.

9. Be not overly concerned in another man's business, and what is of no concern to you, avoid.

10. ' In tribulation be patient and humble yourself under the mighty hand of God, with these thoughts foremost in your mind: first, that it is God who chasteneth; second, it is for your good; third, God will ease the burden; fourth, He will give you strength to endure; fifth, He will deliver from affliction at an expedient time.

11. Never consider any sin as small or of no account, because every sin, though it seem ever so small, is a transgression against God. A small sin that is loved and nurtured can condemn a man as well as a gross sin. A small leak, if not repaired, can sink a ship in time;

likewise a small sin if continued without repentance can sink a soul and send it to hell. Beware, then, not only of great sins but also of small. Make a habit of overcoming every small temptation, and you can be master over great ones, too. Especially shun willful sinning, that ye provoke not God to anger; for of a truth it is hard to obtain forgiveness for sins that were willfully committed.

12. "Rejoice not when your enemy falleth" (Prov. 24:17). What happens to another today may happen to you tomorrow, and he who rejoices at the calamities of another shall not go unpunished. Prov. 17:5.

13. Permit not envy or hatred in your heart, nor carry a grudge against anyone. God loved us when we were His enemies and therefore He expects us to love our enemies for His sake. It is but a small thing for us to forgive our enemies, in comparison to what God has forgiven us. Even though you may think your enemy unworthy of your

forgiveness it is well worth doing it for Christ's sake.

14. Do not think any less of a godly and holy life because it is held in contempt by the unsaved. For the same reason do not forget the gravity of sin just because it is so widespread and most people live a sinful life. Righteousness and the majority are not always on the same side. The way to hell is always full of wandering souls. Matt. 7:13. If God should ask you on the Judgment Day, "Why did you desecrate the Sabbath? Why did you indulge in drunkenness? Why were you dishonest? Why did you pass your time in hating and jealousies?" Would you then answer, "Lord, I did so because almost everyone else did so."? This will be of all answers the least worthy, and God will say, "Because you have sinned with the majority, you will go to hell with the majority."

15. If you have an important decision to make, or you find yourself in circum-

stances where you know not what is best to do or answer, spend at least one night in meditation. You will not be sorry.

16. Never go to sleep without considering how you have spent the day just past, what you accomplished for good or evil, and you will readily perceive whether you are using your time—fleeting, unredeemabe time—in a constructive manner or not.

Rules of a Godly Life
Part II

Part Two: WORDS

1. Think! For every idle word you speak you must give account thereof in the day of judgment. Matt. 12:36. "In the multitude of words there wanteth not sin" (Prov. 10:19). Seek to avoid, therefore, all non-edifying talk; let your words be thoughtful, few, and true. Consider beforehand if what you are about to say is worth saying. Practice saying much with few words. Never

present a tale as true unless you know for certain that it is so; it is better to say nothing at all than to say something that may turn out to be false or otherwise of no value.

For once it becomes known that you are not conscientious to always speak only the truth, no one will believe you even when you do speak the truth. If, however, you have great respect for the truth your every word will carry more weight than those spoken under oath by a liar.

2. If you desire in honorable company to be joyful take care that your merriment prove worthy of Christian love, purity, and respectability. Avoid, therefore, rude insults, mocking speech, indecent words, and filthy jokes of which respectable people would be ashamed. First, because lewd conversation of this sort is outward proof of an unregenerate heart; "For out of the abundance of the heart the mouth speaketh" (Matt. 12: 34). Second, because smutty humor and

immodest words smooth the road to dishonorable deeds.

Yet you may say, "One must have something to say when in company with his friends to pass the time and to delight each other." This is indeed a wretched excuse. Such mirth is clearly forbidden by God's Word, "Neither filthiness, nor foolish talking, nor jesting, which are not convenient," says the Apostle Paul, are to be permitted. "For because of these things cometh the wrath of God upon the children of disobedience" (Eph. 5:4, 6). Through such evil talk and vain mirth the Holy Spirit of God is grieved. Eph. 4:29-30.

The tongue is the glory of man and the honor of the body. Shall it then be misused in unwholesome speech? When the tongue becomes corrupt it defileth the whole body filling it with unrighteousness. See James 3:6. Loath all filthiness; let your speech be always full of love and to the edification of those who hear you, that they may be strengthened thereby. Use the gift of speech as a means of rebuking the idle, of instructing the ignorant, and of comforting the troubled. God will reward you with a fuller measure of His gifts. See Mark 4:25.

3. Be especially diligent to keep free from the vulgar thoughtless habit of swearing and the profane use of the holy name of God. It is indisputable evidence of a frivolous, impious, and ungodly character. It is also true that he who seeks with oaths to add strength and truth to his words is seldom a man of integrity; for if he has no scruples against misusing God's name why should one suppose that he has any conscience against lying? "But let your communication be, Yea, yea; Nay, nay: for whatsoever is more than these cometh of evil" (Matt. 5:37). And that you might the better avoid profaneness, seek not the companionship of the profane, where you, too, may through familiarity fall into the habit. Rebuke

a friend for profaneness, if he accepts it; if not, there is no gain in rebuking. See Proverbs 9:8.

4. Be not too ready to believe everything you hear, and do not repeat everything you hear, lest in this way you lose a friend and gain an enemy. When you hear complaint or gossip about another, thoroughly investigate the actual circumstances before offering your criticism or passing your opinion.

5. Confide to no one your personal secrets unless you have beforehand found him to be worthy of your trust. Here is one way to prove him and learn to know him well: confide to him some secret of small importance; if he keeps it to himself it is an indication of his trustworthiness. However it is not wise to inform any friend carelessly of all your secrets. There is a possibility that at some later time you may have sharp differences and then he may use his knowledge to your harm.

6. Do not speak evil of friends; rath-

er, speak well of them wherein they deserve praise. What is not praiseworthy keep to yourself. Slanderings and scornful gossip are poison to any friendship. If you are present when others speak disrespectfully of one who is absent, search first your own heart before joining in; without doubt you will find there the same (or greater) shortcomings. This should move you to better yourself, and yet keep you from speaking evil of others and belittling them.

7. When you need advice do not seek a counselor on the basis of his prestige or esteem among the people. Go to those who have experience in that concerning which you seek counsel. For if a man accustomed to recognition above his fellows gives you advice, and you do not comply with his recommendations because you feel they are impractical for you, he may be insulted and become your enemy.

8. If someone with good intentions gives you advice which turns out to be

not good, do not hold it against him. For even a good counsel sometimes fails, and there is no one on earth who can tell what the future holds. No one is wise enough or has foresight enough to do so. Do not scoff at the advice of unaccomplished brethren who have your welfare at heart.

9. Do not make fun of another's weaknesses. Instead, think of your own shortcomings. Gal. 6. We all have our weak points, and there is none of whom others say not, "O that this or that were different." Either we are, or have been, or may become subject to most anything, even as others. Therefore show patience and sympathy toward your brother's weaknesses and mistakes. At the same time, do not strengthen him in sin by your nonchalance or by neglecting brotherly admonitions and reproof. If you wish to admonish a brother be careful to bring your reproof at a suitable time; for a reproof at the wrong time may easily

do more harm than good, especially if the rebuke is too sharp or not tempered with gentleness. A reproof is like a salad, it needs more oil than vinegar.

10. Make a habit of not discussing or judging another's words unless you know you have heard and understood aright what they meant to say.

11. You cannot have disputes and divisions with fellow humans and still have peace with God. If you love God, you must also love your fellow men, because God has commanded it.

12. Patiently bear your cross without complaining; for your adversary may rejoice at your discomfiture, and others will think less of you.

13. Consider him a friend who rebukes you privately. It is a pitiful state-of-affairs indeed, for a man to have no one who dares to correct him when he has need of it. For such a man is likely to think he makes no mistakes if he receives no reproof, and will live on in error to his own destruction. Whereas,

this might be prevented by an earnest appeal from a friend.

Everyone most certainly needs instruction at times. The eye sees all and seeks the improvement of all, but it cannot see itself to aid its own improvement. Thus it is with us—we are so prejudiced in our own favor that we cannot see our own mistakes and shortcomings as easily as those of others. Therefore, it is very necessary that we have their help, since they can see our needs much more clearly than we ourselves can. Regardless whether reproof is given justly or unjustly, whether it comes from a friend or an enemy, it can do a wise and understanding person no harm; for if it be well-grounded it is a reminder to better himself, and if it be false it can serve as a warning of what to shun. If you are a person who can not bear reproof, your only choice is to never do anything wrong.

Rules of a Godly Life
Part III
Part Three: WORKS

1. Do no evil, even if it is in thy power to do so. Do nothing in secret of which you would need to be ashamed before men. Remember with Joseph that, though no man sees, God sees all; and that your conscience will testify against you. Abhor all sins, not alone those that are apparent to others, but also secret sins. For even as God is a righteous God, so will He, if you do not repent, bring all your hidden sins to light. I Cor. 4:5; Ps. 50:21.

2. Stand firm, with all your strength, against your bosom sins, those which your personal nature, more than any other sin, has a tendency to commit. One man loves the honor of men; another has a love for money; a third may tend to drunkenness; a fourth to the sins of the flesh; a fifth to pride, etc.

Against your strongest evil inclinations you must above all others defend yourself, for if you overcome them you can easily master other temptations. As a fowler retains control of birds by one leg, so has Satan that man in his power who succumbs to one temptation, and this as fully as if he fell to all.

3. If you desire to avoid sin you will need to shun every occasion and opportunity that tends to evil-doing. He who does not avoid the conditions that lead to evil can not expect to overcome sin. Evil companions lead to sin, such as those from whom one hears indecent speech, by which he may easily be misled and corrupted. Bad company ruins good morals. I Cor. 15:33. Evil associations are the Devil's drag-net, with which he draws many to perdition. Avoid conpanionship with ungodly, lewd persons. "If sinners entice you, do not consent" (Prov. 1:10, RSV). Those who spend much time with sinful companions are easily corrupted by them,

adopting their habits of speech and becoming similar in character ere they realize it. Evil companions demand conformity. In their company one must either sin or suffer scorn. With this in mind a devout man avoids the company of the wicked. If you do not wish to be enticed to fornication and impurity, flee diligently from occasions and persons where the door to these sins would be open. To escape drunkenness (which is the broad way to hell), seek not the comradeship of a drunkard, and look not to him as friend. For of what help is such a friend who may ruin your life, yea destroy your salvation? For experience teaches that more people are killed by friends by way of drunkenness than are slain by the swords of enemies. More people have perished by wine than have been drowned in water. Beware of all allurements to sin! You know not how soon you may be ensnared by Satan and sin.

4. When you are tempted by others

or by your own impulse, to do harm to a fellowman, pause to consider how you would feel if others did so to you. Do nothing to others that you would not wish them to do to you. "All things whatsoever ye would that men should do to you, do ye even so to them." Matt. 7:12. What you yourself dislike do not to others. . . .

5. When you in your calling face a great undertaking do not lose faith in the power of God to provide. Begin nothing without first praying for God's blessing, for without His sanction all our cares and labors are in vain. Ps. 127:1-2. On the blessings of God depend all things. Pray the Lord to bless your labors, and then proceed to the task at hand with joyful spirit, committing all to the wise providence of God, who cares for us and supplies the needs of those who fear Him.

6. Do not attempt supporting yourself in any occupation forbidden by

God. For to what advantage is wealth won at the expense of your soul? Matt. 16:26. Even though you may make great temporal gains through dishonesty, you will thereby forfeit the blessing of a clear conscience. Who can bear the burden of a disturbed, nagging conscience? Be diligent, therefore, as was the Apostle Paul, always taking pains to have a clear conscience towards God and towards men. Acts 24:16.

7. Do not be proud and overbearing because you have been blessed with this world's goods, or with outstanding personality features; for God who has given can also take away, and may do so if you through pride or contempt of others make misuse of His gifts to you. Even though you possess certain qualities of which you may feel proud, they are more than offset by your many bad habits and shortcomings which prove you unworthy in your own eyes. He who knows himself well is certain to find enough of human frailty to make

it extremely difficult for him to consider himself better than others.

8.   Be a true servant of Christ, not only by attending church services or by taking part in religious ceremonies, but throughout every area of your life, shunning all sin, and with a true obedient spirit obeying all the commandments of God. Be not satisfied with a reputation for godliness: let your character be equally good. Woe unto the man who is not pious yet wants to be considered as such.

9.   Do not think that it will suffice to only serve God yourself, and not see to it that all in your care do likewise. The duty of every father lies not alone in personal service to God, but also in influencing his family and servants to do likewise. God has commanded, "And these words, which I command thee this day, shall be in thine heart: and thou shalt teach them diligently unto thy children, and shalt talk of them when thou sittest in thine house,

and when thou walkest by the way, and when thou liest down, and when thou risest up." Deut. 6:6, 7. So did Joshua, the gallant God-fearing hero, informing the people of Israel that whether or not they served the Lord, he and his house would do so. Josh. 24:15. A father is as accountable for the welfare of those in his house as a government for her charge or a pastor for his flock. He must therefore be deeply concerned that his entire household truly worship and serve God, which is the only way for them to obtain salvation.

10. Detest idleness as a pillow of Satan and a cause of all sorts of wickedness, and be diligent in your appointed tasks that you be not found idle. Satan has great power over the idle, to lead them into many sins. King David was idle on the rooftop of his house when he fell into adultery. II Sam. 11:2-5.

11. Practice modesty in the wearing of clothes, and have nothing to do with

pomp and luxury in raiment. It is great vanity to spend as much on one suit as would ordinarily be required to clothe two or three persons. When you become old and think back to the time when you sought to adorn yourself, you will feel only regret that you once loved such vain display. Read much in God's Word and you will find many warnings against pride. No other sin was punished more severely. Pride changed angels to devils. A once powerful king, Nebuchadnezzar, was transformed into a brute beast [to eat grass like an ox]. And Jezebel (a dominant queen) was eaten of dogs as the result of her pride. II Kings 9:30-37.

12.   Do nothing in anger but consider well before you act, lest you be sorry later and will acquire a name of evil repute. In time your anger will cool and you will be able to decide wisely what has to be done. Make a difference between one who has wronged you against his will through lack of fore-

thought, and one who has deliberately and maliciously done so. Be gracious to the former and let your reactions toward the latter be tempered with righteousness.

13. Be not too intimate with any man, except he fear God; for it is certain that any and all friendships, however established, built on any other foundation than the fear of God, may not last long.

14. For the sake of their friendship it is best for friends not to become too confidential; for this life is so filled with change and circumstances that it is hard for any man to retain the good will of all his friends unto the end of his days.

15. If you chance to fall into any kind of dispute with a friend, do not despise him for this reason, nor betray his confidences. Prov. 11:13. In this way you may win him again as a friend.

16. No one is his own master, only a steward of that which is in his care.

Therefore give of your goods to the poor and needy, wisely, willingly, and heartily. 12:13; II Cor. 9:7.

17. Preside over those in your charge with kindness and meekness, rather than to subject them to fear and terror. . . . The righteousness of God can not long endure tyranny; an oppressor does not rule long. An overly severe administration of justice is gross unrighteousness. God requires meekness and humility of those in authority as well as justice. Therefore govern your subjects with love and mercy, so that they will love you more than fear you.

18. Finally, be friendly to all and a burden to no one. Live holy before God; before yourself, moderately; before your neighbors, honestly. Let your life be modest and reserved, your manner courteous, your admonitions friendly, your forgiveness willing, your promises true, your speech wise, and share gladly the bounties you receive.

MENNONITE CONFESSION OF FAITH*

ADOPTED IN THE CITY OF DORT, HOLLAND, IN 1632

ARTICLE I.

Concerning God and the Creation of All Things

Whereas it is declared, that "without faith it is impossible to please God" (Heb. 11:6), and that "he that cometh to God must believe that he is, and that he is a rewarder of them that diligently seek him," therefore we confess with the mouth, and believe with the heart, together with all the pious, according to the Holy Scriptures, that there is one eternal, almighty, and incomprehensible God, Father, Son, and the Holy Ghost, and none more and none other, before

---

*This confession was written and adopted at a Peace Convention held at Dortretcht, on the 21st day of April, 1632, entitled: A Declaration of the Chief Articles of our General Christian Faith.

whom no God existed, neither will exist after him. For from him, through him, and in him are all things. To him be blessing, praise, and honor, for ever and ever. Gen. 17:1; Deut. 6:4; Isaiah 46:9; I John 5:7.

In this one God, who "worketh all in all," we believe. Him we confess as the Creator of all things, visible and invisible; who in six days created and prepared "heaven and earth, and the sea, and all things that are therein." And we further believe, that this God still governs and preserves the same, together with all his works, through his wisdom, his might, and the "word of his power." Gen 5:1,2; Acts 14:15; I Cor. 12:6; Heb. 1:3.

When he had finished his works and, according to his good pleasure, had ordained and prepared each of them, so that they were right and good according to their nature, being and quality, he created the first man, Adam, and father of all of us, gave him a body formed "of the dust of the ground, and breathed into his nostrils the breath of life," so that he "became a living soul," created by God in his own "image and likeness," in "righteousness and true holiness" unto eternal life. He also gave him a place above all other creatures and endowed him with many high and excellent gifts, put him into the garden of Eden, and gave him a commandment and an interdiction. Thereupon he took a rib from the side of Adam, made a woman out of it, brought her to him, and gave her to him as a helpmeet and housewife. Consequently he has caused, that from this first man, Adam, all men who "dwell on the face of the earth," have been begotten and have descended. Gen. 1:27; 2:7, 15, 17, 22; 5:1; Acts 17:26.

ARTICLE II.
The Fall of Man

We believe and confess, that, according to the purport of the Holy Scrip-

tures, our first parents, Adam and Eve,
did not long remain in the happy state
in which they were created; but did,
after being seduced by the deceit and
"subtilty" of the serpent, and envy of
the devil, violate the high command of
God, and became disobedient to their
Creator; through which disobedience
"sin entered into the world, and death
by sin;" so that "death passed upon all
men, for that all have sinned," and
thereby incurred the wrath of God and
condemnation. For which reason our
first parents were, by God, driven out of
Paradise, to cultivate the earth, to maintain themselves thereon in sorrow, and
to "eat their bread in the sweat of their
face," until they "returned to the
ground, from which they were taken."
And that they did, therefore, through
this one sin, so far apostatize, depart,
and estrange themselves from God, that
they could neither help themselves, nor
be helped by any of their descendants,
nor by angels, nor by any other creature

in heaven or on earth, nor be redeemed or reconciled to God; but would have had to be lost forever, had not God, who pitied his creatures, in mercy, interposed in their behalf, and made provision for their restoration. Gen. 3: 6,23; Rom. 5:12-19; Psa. 47:8,9; Rev. 5:3; John 3:16.

ARTICLE III.

The Restoration of Man through the Promise of the Coming Christ

Regarding the restoration of our first parents and their descendants, we believe and confess: That God, notwithstanding their fall, transgression and sin, and although they had no power to help themselves, he was nevertheless not willing that they should be cast off entirely, or be eternally lost; but again called them unto him, comforted them, and showed them that there were yet means with him for their reconciliation; namely, the immaculate Lamb, the Son of God; who "was foreordained" to this purpose "before the foundation of the world," and who was promised to them and all their descendants, while they (our first parents) were yet in paradise, for their comfort, redemption, and salvation; yea, who was given to them thenceforward, through faith, as their own; after which all the pious patriarchs, to whom this promise was often renewed, longed and searched, beholding it through faith at a distance, and expecting its fulfillments—expecting that he (the Son of God), would, at his coming, again redeem and deliver the fallen race of man from their sins, their guilt, and unrighteousness. John 1:29; 11:27; I Pet. 1:19; Gen. 3:15; I John 2:1, 2; 3:8; Gal. 4:4, 5.

ARTICLE IV.
The Advent of Christ into this World, and the Reason for His Coming

We believe and confess further: That "when the fullness of the time was come," after which all the pious patriarchs so ardently longed, and which they so anxiously awaited—the previously promised Messiah, Redeemer, and Saviour, proceeded from God, being sent by him, and, according to the prediction of the prophets and the testimony of the evangelists, came into the world, yea, into the flesh, so that the Word itself thus became flesh and man; and that he was conceived by the Virgin Mary (who was espoused to a man named Joseph, of the house of David), and that she bare him as her first born son at Bethlehem, "wrapped him in swaddling clothes, and laid him in a manger." John 4:25; 16:28; I Tim. 3:16; Matt. 1:21; John 1:14; Luke 2:7.

Further, we believe and confess, that this is the same One, "whose goings forth have been from of old, from everlasting;" who has neither beginning of days, nor end of life." Of whom it is testified, that he is "Alpha and Omega, the beginning and the end, the first and the last." That this is also he—and none

other—who was chosen, promised, and
sent; who came into the world; and who
is God's only, first, and proper Son;
who was before the world; yea, who
was David's Lord, and who is God of
the "whole earth," "the firstborn of
every creature;" who was sent into the
world, and himself delivered up the
body prepared for him, as "an offering
and a sacrifice to God for a sweet smell-
ing savor," yea, for the comfort, redemption, and salvation of all—of the
human race. Micah 5:2; Heb. 7:3;
Rev. 1:8; John 3:16; Rom. 8:32; Col.
1:15; Heb. 10:5.

But how, or in what manner, this
worthy body was prepared, or how the
Word became flesh, and he himself
man, we content ourselves with the declaration which the faithful evangelists
have given and left in their description
thereof; according to which we confess
with all the saints, that he is the Son of
the living God, in whom exist all our
hope, comfort, redemption, and salva-

tion, and which we are to seek in no one else. Luke 1:31-35; John 30:31.

Further, we believe and confess by authority of scripture, that when he had ended his course, and "finished" the work for which he was sent into the world, he was, by the providence of God, delivered into the hands of the unrighteous; suffered under the governor, Pontius Pilate, was crucified, died, was buried, rose again from the dead on the third day, and ascended into heaven, where he now sits at the right hand of the Majesty of God on high;" and from whence he will come again to judge the living and the dead. Luke 23:1; 33:53; 24:5, 6, 51.

Thus we believe the Son of God died —"tasted death for every man," shed his precious blood, and thereby bruised the head of the serpent, destroyed the works of the devil, "blotted out the hand-writing," and purchased redemption for the whole human race; and thus he became the source of eternal

salvation to all who from the time of
Adam to the end of the world, shall
have believed in him, and obeyed him.
Gen. 3:15; I John 3:8; Col. 2:14;
Rom. 5:18.

ARTICLE V.

Then Law of Christ, which is the Holy Gospel, or the New Testament

We also believe and confess, that
Christ, before his ascension, established
and instituted his New Testament and
left it to his followers, to be and remain
an everlasting testament, which he confirmed and sealed with his own precious
blood; and in which he has so highly
commended to them, that neither men
nor angels may change it, neither take
therefrom nor add thereto. Jer. 31:31;
Heb. 9:15-17; Matt. 26:28; Gal. 1:8;
I Tim. 6:3; Rev. 22:18, 19; Matt.
5:18; Luke 21:33.

And that he caused this Testament
(in which the whole counsel and will
of his heavenly Father, so far as these

are necessary to the salvation of man, are comprehended), to be proclaimed, in his name, through his beloved apostles, messengers, and servants (whom he chose and sent into all the world for this purpose)—to all nations, people and tongues; these apostles preaching repentance and remission of sins; and that he, in said Testament, caused it to be declared, that all men without distinction, if they are obedient, through faith, follow, fulfill and live according to the precepts of the same, are his children and rightful heirs; having thus excluded none from the precious inheritance of eternal salvation, except the unbelieving and disobedient, the headstrong and unconverted; who despise such salvation; and thus by their own actions incur guilt by refusing the same, and "judge themselves unworthy of everlasting life." Mark 16:15; Luke 24:46, 47; Rom. 8:17; Acts 13:46.

ARTICLE VI.

Repentance and Amendment of Life

We believe and confess, that, as the "imagination of man's heart is evil from his youth," and consequently inclined to all unrighteousness, sin and wickedness, that, therefore, the first doctrine of the precious New Testament of the Son of God is, Repentance and amendment of life. Gen. 8:21; Mark 1:15. Therefore those who have ears to hear, and hearts to understand, must "bring forth fruits meet for repentance," amend their lives, believe the gospel, "depart from evil and do good," desist from wrong and cease from sinning, "put off the old man with his deeds, and put on the new man, which after God is created in righteousness and true holiness." For neither **Baptism, Sacrament, nor Church Fellowship,** nor any other external ceremony, can, without faith, the new birth, and a change or renewal of life, help, or qualify us, that we may please God, or receive any consolation or promise of salvation from him. Luke 3:8; Eph. 4:22, 24; Col. 3:9, 10. But on the contrary, we must go to God "with a sincere heart in full assurance of faith," and believe in Jesus Christ, as the scriptures speak and testify of him. Through which faith we obtain the pardon of our sins, become sanctified, justified, and children of God; yea, partakers of his mind, nature and image, as we are born again of God through his incorruptible seed from above. Heb. 10:21, 22; John 7:38; II Pet. 1:4.

ARTICLE VII.—Holy Baptism

Regarding baptism, we confess that all penitent believers, who through faith, the new birth and renewal of the Holy Ghost, have become united with God, and whose names are recorded in heaven, must, on such scriptural confession of their faith, and renewal of life, according to the command and doctrine of Christ and, the example and custom of the apostles be baptized with water in

the ever adorable name of the Father,
and of the Son, and of the Holy Ghost,
to the burying of their sins, and thus be
become incorporated into the communion of the saints; whereupon they
must learn to observe all things what-
ever the Son of God taught, left on re-
cord, and commanded his followers to
do. Matt. 3:15; 28:19, 20; Mark 16:
15, 16; Acts 2:38; 8:12, 38; 9:19;
10:47; 16:33; Rom. 6:3, 4; Col. 2:12.

ARTICLE VIII.
The Church of Christ

We believe in and confess a visible
Church of God, consisting of those,
who, as before remarked, have truly re-
pented, and rightly believed; who are
rightly baptized, united with God in
heaven, and incorporated into the communion of the saints on earth. I Cor.
12:13. And these, we confess, are a
"chosen generation, a royal priesthood,
an holy nation," who have the testimony that they are the "bride" of
Christ; yea, that they are children and

heirs of eternal life—a "habitation of God through the Spirit," built on the foundation of the apostles and prophets, of which "Christ himself is the chief corner stone"—the foundation on which his church is built. John 3:29; Matt. 16:18; Eph. 2:19-21; Tit. 3:7; I Pet. 1:18, 19; 2:9. This church of the living God, which he has purchased and redeemed through his own precious blood, and with which he will be—according to his own promise—for her comfort and protection, "always, even unto the end of the world" yea, will dwell and walk with her, and preserve her, that no "winds" nor "floods," yea, not even the "gates of hell shall prevail against her"—may be known by her evangelical faith, doctrine, love, and godly conversation; also by her pure walk and practice, and her observance of the true ordinances of Christ, which he has strictly enjoined on his followers. Matt. 7:25; 16:18; 28:20; II Cor. 6:16.

ARTICLE IX.

The Office of Teachers and Ministers— Male and Female—in the Church

Regarding the officers, and election of persons to the same, in the church, we believe and confess: That, as the church cannot exist and prosper, nor continue in its structure, without officers and regulations, that therefore the Lord Jesus has himself (as a father in his house), appointed and prescribed his offices and ordinances, and has given commandments concerning the same, as to how each one should walk therein, give heed to his own work and calling, and do it as it becomes him to do. Eph. 4:11, 12. For he himself, as the faithful and great Shepherd, and Bishop of our souls, was sent into the world, not to wound, to break or destroy the souls of men, but to heal them; to seek that which is lost, and to pull down the hedges and partition wall, so as to make out of many one; thus collecting out of Jews and heathen, yea, out of all nations, a church in his name; for which (so that no one might go astray or be lost) he laid down his own life, and thus procured for them salvation, made them free and redeemed them, to which blessing no one could help them, or be of service in obtaining it. I Pet. 2:25; Matt. 18:11; Eph. 2:13, 14; John 10:9, 11, 15.

And that he, besides this, left his church before his departure, provided with faithful ministers, apostles, evangelists, pastors, and teachers, whom he had chosen by prayer and supplic[ation] through the Holy Spi[rit] might govern the chu[rch] watch over, maintain same; yea, do in all them an example, t[a] commanded them, t[o] to teach the church t[o] whatsoever he comm 4:11; Luke 6:12, 28:20.

Also that the apo[stles]

wards, as faithful followers of Christ
and leaders of the church, diligent in
these matters, namely, in choosing
through prayer and supplication to God,
brethren who were to provide all the
churches in the cities and circuits, with
bishops, pastors, and leaders, and to
ordain to these offices such men as took
"heed unto themselves and unto the
doctrine," and also unto the flock; who
were sound in the faith, pious in their
life and conversation and who had—
as well within the church as "without"
good reputation and a good report;
ght be a light and ex-
ness and good works;
dminister the Lord's
ism and sacrament—
e brethren sent by the
lso, at all places, where
had, appoint faithful
who were able to teach
hem in the name of the
laying on of hands,"
ders) were to take care

of all things of which the church stood in need; so that they, as faithful servants, might well "occupy" their Lord's money, gain thereby, and thus "save themselves and those who hear them." I Tim. 3:1; 4:14-16; Acts 1: 23 24; Tit. 1:5; Luke 19:13.

That they should also take good care (particularly each one of the charge over which he had oversight), that all the circuits should be well provided with almoners, who should have the care and oversight of the poor, and who were to receive gifts and alms, and again faithfully to distribute them amongst the poor saints who were in need, and this in all honesty, as is becoming. Acts 6:3-6.

Also that honorable old widows should be chosen as servants, who, besides, the almoners, are to visit, comfort, and take care of the poor, the weak, the afficted, and the needy, as also to visit, comfort, and take care of widows and orphans, and further to assist in taking care of any matters in the church that properly come within their sphere, according to their best ability. I Tim. 5:9, 10; Rom. 16:1, 2.

And as it further regards the almoners, that they (particularly if they are fit persons, and chosen and ordained thereto by the church), may also in aid and relief of the bishops, exhort the church (being, as already remarked, chosen thereto), and thus assist in word and doctrine; so that each one may serve the other from love, with the gift which he has received from the Lord; so that through the common service and assistance of each member, according to his ability, the body of Christ may be edified, and the Lord's vineyard and church be preserved in its growth and structure. II Tim. 2:2.

ARTICLE X.

The Lord's Supper

We also believe in and observe the breaking of bread, or the Lord's Supper,

as the Lord Jesus instituted the same
(with bread and wine) before his sufferings, and also observed and ate it
with the apostles, and also commanded
it to be observed to his remembrance, as
also the apostles subsequently taught
and observed the same in the church,
and commanded it to be observed by believers in commemoration of the death
and sufferings of the Lord—the breaking of his worthy body and the shedding
of his precious blood—for the whole
human race. So is the observance of
this sacrament also to remind us of the
benefit of the said death and sufferings
of Christ, namely, the redemption and
eternal salvation which he purchased
thereby, and the great love thus shown
to sinful man; whereby we are earnestly
exhorted also to love one another—to
love our neighbor—to forgive and ab-
solve him—even as Christ has done unto us—and also to endeavor to maintain and keep alive the union and communion which we have with God, and

amongst one another; which is thus shown and represented to us by the aforesaid breaking of bread. Matt. 26:26; Mark 14:22; Luke 22:19; Acts 2:42, 46; I Cor. 10:16; 11:23-26.

ARTICLE XI.
The Washing of the Saints' Feet

We also confess a washing of the feet of the saints, as the Lord Jesus did not only institute and command the same, but did also himself wash the feet of the apostles, although he was their Lord and master; thereby giving an example that they also should wash one another's feet, and thus do to one another as he did to them; which they also afterwards taught believers to observe, and all this as a sign of true humiliation; but yet more particularly as a sign to remind us of the true washing—the washing and purification of the soul in the blood of Christ. John 13:4-17; I Tim. 5:10.

ARTICLE XII.
Matrimony

We also confess that there is in the

church of God an "honorable" state of matrimony between two believers of the different sexes, as God first instituted the same in paradise between Adam and Eve, and as the Lord Jesus reformed it by removing all abuses which had crept into it, and restoring it to its first order. Gen. 1:27; 2:18, 22, 24.

In this manner the apostle Paul also taught and permitted matrimony in the church, leaving it to each one's own choice to enter into matrimony with any person who would unite with him in such a state, provided that it was done "in the Lord," according to the primitive order; the words "in the Lord," to be understood, according to our opinion, that just as the patriarchs had to marry amongst their own kindred or generation, so there is also no other liberty allowed to believers under the New Testament Dispensation, than to marry amongst the "chosen generation," or the spiritual kindred of Christ;

that is, to such—and none others—as are already, previous to their marriage, united to the church in heart and soul, have received the same baptism, belong to the same church, are of the same faith and doctrine, and lead the same course of life, with themselves. I Cor. 7; 9:5; Gen. 24:4; 28:6; Num. 36:6-9. Such are then, as already remarked, united by God and the church according to the primitive order, and this is then called, "Marrying in the Lord." I Cor. 7:39.

ARTICLE XIII.
The Office of Civil Government

We also believe and confess, that God has instituted civil government, for the punishment of the wicked and the protection of the pious; and also further, for the purpose of governing the world —governing countries and cities; and also to preserve its subjects in good order and under good regulations. Wherefore we are not permitted to despise, blaspheme, or resist the same;

but are to acknowledge it as a minister
of God and be subject and obedient
to it, in all things that do not militate
against the law, will and commandments of God; yea, "to be ready to
every good work;" also faithfully to
pay it custom, tax, and tribute; thus
giving it what is its due; as Jesus Christ
taught, did himself. and commanded
his followers to do. That we are also to
pray to the Lord earnestly for the
government and its welfare, and in behalf of our country, so that we may live
under its protection, maintain ourselves,
and "lead a quiet and peaceable life in
all godliness and honesty." And further,
that the Lord would recompense them
(our rulers), here and in eternity, for all
the benefits, liberties, and favors which
we enjoy under their laudable administration. Rom. 13:1-7; Tit. 3:1, 2; I Pet.
2:17; Matt. 17:27; 22:21; I Tim. 2:1,
2.

ARTICLE XIV.

Defense by Force

Regarding revenge, whereby we resist our enemies with the sword, we believe and confess that the Lord Jesus has forbidden his disciples and followers all revenge and resistance, and has thereby commanded them not to "return evil for evil, nor railing for railing;" but to "put up the sword into the sheath," or, as the prophets foretold, "beat them into ploughshares." Matt. 5:39, 44; Rom. 12:14; I Pet. 3: 9; Isaiah 2:4; Micah 4:3.

From this we see, that, according to the example, life, and doctrine of Christ, we are not to do wrong, or cause offense or vexation to any one; but to seek the welfare and salvation of all men; also, if necessity should require it, to flee, for the Lord's sake, from one city or country to another, and suffer, the "spoiling of our goods," rather than give occasion of offense to any one; and if we are struck on the "right cheek, rather to turn the other also," than revenge ourselves, or return the blow. Matt. 5:39; 10:23; Rom. 12:19.

And that we are, besides this, also to pray for our enemies, comfort and feed them, when they are hungry or thirsty, and thus by well-doing convince them and overcome the evil with good. Rom. 12:20, 21.

Finally, that we are to do good in all respects, "commending ourselves to every man's conscience in the sight of God," and according to the law of Christ, do nothing to others that we would not wish them to do unto us. II Cor. 4:2; Matt. 7:12; Luke 6:31.

ARTICLE XV.
The Swearing of Oaths

Regarding the swearing of oaths, we believe and confess, that the Lord Jesus has dissuaded his followers from and forbidden them the same; that is, that he commanded them to "swear not at all," but that their "Yea" should be "yea" and their "Nay nay." From which we understand that all oaths, high and low, are forbidden; and that instead of them we are to confirm all our promises and covenants, declarations and testimonies of all matters, merely with "Yea that is yea," and "Nay that is nay;" and that we are to perform and fulfill at all times, and in all things, to every one, every promise and obligation to which we thus affirm, as faithfully as if we had confirmed it with the most solemn oath. And if we thus do, we have confidence that no one—not even the government itself—will have just cause to require more of us. Matt. 5:34-37; James 5:12, II Cor. 1:17.

ARTICLE XVI.
Excommunication or Expulsion from the Church

We also believe in and acknowledge the ban, or excommunication, a separation or spiritual punishment by the church, for the amendment, and not for the destruction, of offenders; so that what is pure may be separated from that which is impure. That is, if a person, after having been enlightened, and received the knowledge of the truth, and has been received into the communion of the saints, does willfully, or out of presumption, sin against God or commit some other "sin unto death," thereby falling into such unfruitful works of darkness, that he becomes separated from God, and is debarred from his kingdom—that such an one—when his works are become manifest, and sufficiently known to the church—cannot remain in the "congregation of the righteous;" but must, as an offensive member and open sinner, be excluded from the church, "rebuked before all," and "purged out as leaven," and thus remain until his amendment, as an example and warning to others, and also that the church may be kept pure from such "spots" and "blemishes;" so that not for want of this, the name of the Lord be blasphemed, the church dishonored, and a stumbling-block thrown in the way of those "without," and finally, that the offender may not be condemned with the word, but that he may again be convinced of the error of his ways, and brought to repentance and amendment of life. Isaiah 59:2, I Cor. 5:5, 6, 12; I Tim. 5:20; II Cor. 13:10.

Regarding the brotherly admonition, as also the instruction of the erring, we are to "give all diligence" to watch over them, and exhort them in all meekness to the amendment of their ways (James 5:19, 20); and in case any should remain obstinate and unconverted, to reprove them as the case required. In short, the church must "put away from among herself him that is wicked," wheather it be in doctrine or life.

ARTICLE XVII.
The Shunning of those who are Expelled

As regards the withdrawing from, or the shunning of, those who are expelled, we believe and confess, that if any one, whether it be through a wicked life or perverse doctrine—is so far fallen as to be separated from God, and consequently rebuked by, and expelled from, the church, he must also, according to the doctrine of Christ and his apostles, be shunned and avoided by all the members of the church (particularly by those to whom his misdeeds are known), whether it be in eating or drinking, or other such like social matters. In short, that we are to have noth-nothing to do with him; so that we may not become defiled by intercourse with him, and partakers of his sins; but that he may be made ashamed, be affected in his mind, convinced in his conscience, and thereby induced to amend his ways. I Cor. 5:9-11; Rom. 16:17; II Thess. 3:14; Tit. 3:10.

That nevertheless, as well in shunning as in reproving such offender, such moderation and Christian discretion be used, that such shunning and reproof may not be conducive to his ruin, but be serviceable to his amendment. For should he be in need, hungry, thirsty, naked, sick or visited by some other affliction, we are in duty bound, according to the doctrine and practice of Christ and his apostles, to render him aid and assistance, as necessity may require; otherwise the shunning of him might be rather conducive to his ruin than to his amendment. I Thess. 5:14.

Therefore we must not treat such offenders as enemies, but exhort them as brethren, in order thereby to bring them to a knowledge of their sins and to repentance; so that they may again become reconciled to God and the church, and be received and admitted into the same—thus exercising love towards them, as is becoming. II Thess. 3:15.

ARTICLE XVIII.
The Resurrection of the Dead and the Last Judgment

Regarding the resurrection of the dead, we confess with the mouth, and believe with the heart, that according to the scriptures—all men who shall have died or "fallen asleep," will—through the incomprehensible power of God—at the day of judgment, be "raised up" and made alive; and that these, together with all those who then remain alive, and who shall be "changed in a moment, in the twinkling of an eye, at the last trump," shall "appear before the judgment seat of Christ," where the good shall be separated from the evil, and where "every one shall receive the things done in his body, according to that he hath done, whether it be good or bad;" and that the good or pious shall then further, as the blessed of their Father, be received by Christ into eternal life, where they shall receive that joy which "eye hath not seen, nor ear heard, nor hath entered into the heart of man." Yea, where they shall reign and triumph with Christ forever and ever. Matt. 22:30, 31; 25:31; Dan. 12:2; Job. 19:25, 26; John 5:28, 29; I Cor. 15; I Thess. 4:13.

And that, on the contrary, the wicked or impious, shall, as the accursed of God, be cast into "outer darkness;" yea, into eternal, hellish torments; "where their worm dieth not, and the fire is not quenched," and where—according to Holy Scripture—they can expect no comfort nor redemption throughout eternity. Isaiah 66:24; Matt. 25:46; Mark 9:46; Rev. 14:11.

May the Lord through his grace make us all fit and worthy, that no such calamity may befall any of us; but that we may be diligent, and so take heed to ourselves, that we may be found of him in peace, without spot, and blameless. Amen.

Now these are, as before mentioned, the chief articles of our general Christian Faith, which we everywhere teach in our congregations and families, and according to which we profess to live, and which, according to our convictions, contain the only true Christian Faith, which the apostles in their time believed and taught; yea, which they testified to by their lives and confirmed by their deaths; in which we will also, according to our weakness, gladly abide, live, and die, that at last, together with the apostles and all the pious we may obtain the salvation of our souls through the grace of God.

Thus were the foregoing articles of faith adopted and concluded by our united churches in the city of Dort, in Holland, on the 21st day of April, in the year of our Lord 1632, and signed by the following ministers and teachers.

Dort
Isaac Koenig
Johann Cobryssen
Jan Jacobs
Jacuis Terwen
Claes Dirksen
Mels Gysbaerts
Adrian Cornelis

Flissingen
Dillaert Willeborts
Jacob Pennen
Lieven Marymehr

Utrecht
Herman Segers
Jan Heinrich Hochfeld
Daniel Horens
Abraham Spronk
Wilhelm von Brock-
huysen

Creveldt
Herman op den Graff
Wilhelm Krevnen

Zealand
Cornelius de Moir
Isaac Claes

Armsterdam
Tobias Goverts
Peter Jansen Mayer
Abram Dirks
David ter Haer
Peter Jan von Zingel

Rotterdam
Balten C. Schumacher
Michael Michiels
Israel von Halmael
Heinrich D. Apeldoren
Andreas Lucken

Harlem
John Doom
Peter Gryspeer
D. Wouters Kolenkamp
Peter Joosten

Bommel
Wilhelm J. von Exselt
Gispert Spiering

Schiedam
Cornelis Bom
Lambrecht Paeldink

Gorcum	**Leyden**
Jacob von Sebrecht	Christian de Kopink
Jan J. von Kruysen	Jan Weyns

Arnheim	**Blockzyl**
Cornelis Jans	Claes Claesson
Dirk Renderson	Peter Peterson

Middleburg	**Ziriczee**
Bastian Willemsen	Anton Cornelis
Jan Winkelmans	Peter Jan Zimmerman

From the Upper Country

Peter von Borsel   Anton Hans

Besides this confession being adopted by so many churches, and signed by their ministers, all the churches in Alsace and Germany afterwards adopted it unanimously. Wherefore it was translated from the Holland into the languages of these countries—into French and German—for the use of the churches there, and for others, of which this may serve as a notice.

The following attestation was signed by the brethren in Alsace, who examined this confession and adopted it as their own.

We, the undersigned, ministers of the word of God, and elders of the church in Alsace, hereby declare and make known, that being assembled this 4th of Feb. in the year of our Lord 1660, at Ohnenheim, on account of the Confession of Faith, which was adopted at the Peace Convention in the city of Dort, on the 21st day of April in the year 1632; and having examined the same, and found it, according to our judgment, in agreement with the word of God, we have entirely adopted it as our own. Which we, in testimony of the truth, and a firm faith, have signed with our own hands, as follows:

MINISTERS	ELDERS
Magenheim	**Markirch**
John Miller	Jacob Schmidt
Heidelheim	Bertram Habich
John Ringer	
Baldenheim	**Ohnenheim**
Jacob Schelby	Jacob Gochnauer
Isenheim	**Jepsenheim**
Henry Schneider	John Rudolph Bumen
Kunenheim	**Duerrsanzenheim**
Rudolph Egli	Jacob Schneider
Markirch	**Kunenheim**
Adolph Schmidt	Henry Frick

Postscript to the Foregoing 18 Articles

From an authentic circular letter of the year 1557 from the Highland to the Netherland churches, it appears that from the Eyfelt to Moravia there were 50 churches, of which some consisted of from 500 to 600 brethren. And that there were about that time, at a conference at Strasburg, about 50 preachers and elders present, who discoursed about matters concerning the welfare of the churches.

These leaders of the non-resistant Christians endeavored earnestly to propagate the truth; so that like a "grain of mustrad seed," of small beginning, it grew against all bloody persecution, to the height in which it is to be seen in so many large churches in Germany, Prussia, the Principality of Cleves, etc., and particularly in the United Netherlands.

But finally, alas! there arose disunion amongst them about matters of faith, which so deeply grieved the peaceably disposed amonst them, that they not only thought about means to heal the schism, and restore union, but did also take the matter in hand, and concluded at Cologne, in the year 1591, a laudable peace between the Highland and Netherland churches. Still the schism was not fully healed. Consequently in the years 1628 and 1630, it was deemed necessary at a certain conference, by some lovers of peace to appoint another conference, in order to see whether they could come to an understanding, and the schism be fully healed. Consequently, in order to attain this object in the most effectual manner, there assembled at Dort, from many of the churches in Holland, on the 21st of April, 1632, fifty-one ministers of the word of God, appointed for said purpose; who deemed it advisable that a scriptural confession of faith should be drawn up, to which all parties should adhere, and on which this peace convention and the intended union should be founded and publicly adopted, confirmed, signed, the so much wished for peace, obtained, and the light again put on the candlestick, to the honor of the non-resistant Christianity.

INDEX